Where

CATs

Sleep

Where CATs Sleep

By Liz Ross

Illustrated by Lynn Chang

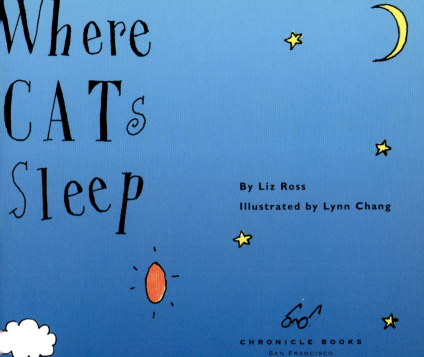

CHRONICLE BOOKS
SAN FRANCISCO

Printed in Hong Kong.

*Text copyright © 1996
by Liz Ross*

*Illustrations copyright © 1996
by Lynn Chang*

Library of Congress Cataloging-in-Publication
Data available.

ISBN: 0-8118-1201-4

Distributed in Canada by Raincoast Books,
8680 Cambie Street
Vancouver, B.C. V6P 6M9

Chronicle Books
275 Fifth Sreet
San Francisco, CA 94103

10 9 8 7 6 5 4 3 2 1

FOR

MICA

AND

MINOU

Every morning, my cat Mica curls up on the morning paper, and every morning I gently remove her. It was during breakfast, sometime during our tenth year together, that I realized this ritual had been going on for as long as she had been with me. Working at home as I do, I can now see there are countless other times throughout the day when we undergo a similar routine.

With accuracy and grace, cats sleep exactly where we wish they wouldn't—and almost always at the most inopportune times. This is but one of the many reasons why we love them, and certainly the inspiration for this book.

On the keyboard
        while you're typing.

On the mantle

upside
down.

Among your

most cherished possessions.

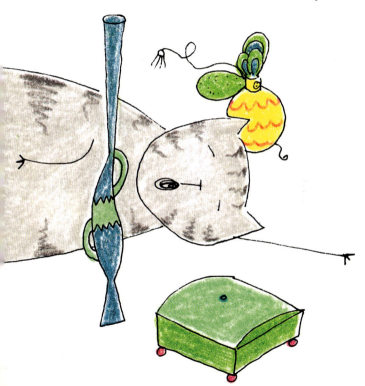

On the clothes

you had ironed

and laid out to wear.

On your shoes.

On the chair you

were about

to sit in.

In the
suitcase
you were
packing.

On your head
while you're
sleeping.

On the table

before dinner.

On the

flowers

you just
planted.

In the laundry basket

while the clothes

are still

warm.

On the
pile of leaves

you were
raking.

On the edge of the windowsill.

In your
drawer.

In the doorway.

On the hood
of your car.

On the bed you were making.

On top of the
T.V.

On

each

other.

Anywhere

they please!